THE LITTLE
BLACK DRESS
OF
FINANCE

Library of Congress Control Number: 2021938768

ISBN: 978-1-7371255-7-0

Armin Lear Press Inc
215 W Riverside Drive, #4362
Estes Park, CO 80517

The Little Black Dress of Finance

CAREN J. LAVERTY

I dedicate this book to my family. My husband, Bill, is forever encouraging and patient with my never-ending financial conversations. No wonder why he gets such a good night's sleep! He's actually the better writer so it amazes me that I'm the one to write a book. Hopefully one day, he'll bless us all with his words.

My daughter, Charlene, is the one who came up with the name for this book. Considering she graduated from Savannah College of Art design with a major in Fibers (textiles) and a minor in Fashion, she is always my go to person for fashion information. She epitomizes beauty and brains. Who better to recommend some Valentino Rockstuds?!

My son, Joseph, is a data analyst and my fellow trading partner. He will gladly partake in daily stock market conversations then act on them! He's also one of the funniest people I know and made me belly laugh describing the conversations of the Reddit WallStreetBets group. One day I'm certain he will use his financial knowledge and savviness to help educate others.

Finally, there's my spoiled third child, our ninety-pound chocolate lab named Jake. What would I do without my handsome boy to love and hug? Never mind the nine hundred tennis ball tosses required on a daily basis.

Contents

INTRODUCTION
The History of the Little Black Dress

Parisian designer Coco Chanel is typically credited with creating the Little Black Dress. In 1926, Vogue magazine displayed a simple black dress in crepe de Chine. It featured long narrow sleeves with a string of pearls. *Vogue* called this Chanel's Ford, meaning that it would be accessible to women of all classes. Later in her career, Coco Chanel said: "I imposed black; it is still going strong today because black wipes out everything else around." The Little Black Dress became a staple in every woman's wardrobe. Of course, in 1961, Audrey Hepburn famously wore a Givenchy little black dress in Breakfast at Tiffany's cited as one of the most iconic items of clothing in the history of the twentieth century.

However, not to take anything away from Ms. Chanel or Ms. Hepburn, but black dresses have been used frequently in the history of art between the fifteenth and nineteenth centuries, according to **A Look into The History of Black Dresses and Why There's Nothing "Little" About Them,** by <u>Yassana Croizat-Glazer</u>. This is a wonderfully interesting article discussing the artful use of the color black in many different perspectives and presentations. She makes note of Catherine de Medici (1519-89) who became regent of France after her husband was killed in a horrible jousting accident. She wore black long after the mourning period to display her Catholic devotion and to demonstrate that she meant business. Of course, she surrounded herself with women in the latest fashions who became known as her "flying squadron." There are also the paintings of Berthe Morisot (1841-95) who was a painter herself and sister-in-law of famous French impressionist Edouard Manet. The use of black dresses in her paintings emphasized her seductiveness as well as the art and imagery around her.

Over centuries of time, there has been a wide range of uses and versatility in the black dress, not just in art. The Church is where the black dress originally attained its status. In Spain, black wedding dresses were traditional and symbolized a bride's devotion to her husband. The white wedding dress didn't become tradition until 1840 when Queen Victoria married Prince Albert. However, black dresses were also worn exclusively by servants and women in mourning. Many women during wartime would wear black when fabric was rationed and would only use an average of seven yards instead of nineteen.

As you can see, no matter what the size and purpose, black dresses have been an elegant part of women's wardrobes over centuries, representing everything from seductiveness, authority, dignity, and strength to mourning and modesty. They are empowering. The classic black dress should be as much a part of your life as the knowledge of your personal finances, which is equally as empowering. Knowledge of your finances should be a staple in your life as much, if not more, than the little black dress in your closet. Our finances are an integral part of every facet of our lives. They affect our everyday lifestyle, our children, and our future. The financial world is no longer a man's world. Wouldn't it be great for women to be the ones teaching their children about finances? Women are making more money, living longer, and running businesses and countries. There's no reason we can't grasp financial terms and manage our investments individually or in unison with our partner. Let's empower each other together while looking good … of course!

CHAPTER 1
WHY SHOULD I CARE?

Ho hum, this stuff is so boring! Why should I care? Why do I need to know this anyway? Too bad the investment world didn't come up with terms like basic body lotion investments, risky red lipstick stocks, or your average hold-everything-handbag balanced fund. Then maybe investments might make sense. As boring as it may seem, having a good understanding of your finances gives you the same sense of security as that handsome hunk of a boyfriend or spouse with his arms wrapped tight around you. From the day you leave your parent's house until the day you turn 100 and every step in between, your finances will have a huge impact on your life. Being financially secure is liberating and stress relieving.

It's all up to you! What choices will you make?

Will you run up massive credit card debt buying 48 pairs of spectacular shoes you just had to have, only to find you can't pay more than the minimum payment every month? That option means you pay a huge amount of interest thereby keeping credit card companies in business and leaving you broke. Will you marry that handsome boyfriend and let him handle the finances until you find out he has a gambling problem, ran off with your best friend, or just isn't very good at it? That option leaves you vulnerable, in the dark, and uneducated. After all, it's your future, isn't it? Maybe you'll just hand your hard-earned money over to Mr. Slick Stockbroker hoping he knows what he's doing. He could take advantage of you in a second by putting you in high-cost investments, having a much riskier plan than your comfort level, or just flat out running off with your money.

The point is you don't need to be an expert, but you do need to have goals, a plan, and know what you own. Know who you are and take charge of your life, don't let someone take charge of you. Before we get started on financial and investing knowledge, it's equally as important to take a good look at yourself and your habits. Sometimes, changing certain habits can be a very important first step in financial security.

P.S. If you know you won't have the money to pay off those shoes when the bill comes, here's a novel idea: Don't buy them! Trust me, I have a shoe fetish, so I know how hard it is. You can do it. There will be another cute pair next month, too. Save your money until you can afford them.

CHAPTER 2
SPENDING, SPENDING, SPENDING

Speaking of spending, let's first address habits that get us into trouble. Everyone loves chocolate cake, right?! It tastes fantastic, so why not eat it every day? How about every meal? What's wrong with having more of a good thing? Wouldn't overindulging in chocolate cake every day make you happy? Maybe at first, but after a while some things might start to bother you. Could it be that your belly would look like a huge squishy piece of cake, you would have holes in your teeth, and or maybe develop an unbreakable sugar addiction? After a while, you'd hate what you've become.

Now how about your spending? Doesn't it feel good to get those new fantastic designer boots? I'll bet you can't wait to wear them out with your new sweater dress, covered by your new camel hair coat. (It does sound like a nice outfit, doesn't it?!) Never mind that this new fabulous outfit caused you to max out yet another credit card. Maybe you can wear it while you plan the next vacation you can't afford or the new living room furniture you just had to have.

Do you continue to spend even though you're on the verge of financial ruin? Well, you're not the only one. Believe it or not, even high-income earners can have massive spending problems. There was even a *Wall Street Journal* article of September 5, 2014 written by Veronica Dagher, "Six-Figure Incomes—and Facing Financial Ruin Some High Earners Live Paycheck to Paycheck. Here's How to Break the Cycle of Overspending."

Dagher tells the story of Sylvia Flores who earned more than $200,000/year yet she ran up some $300,000 in credit-card debt before deciding to put her financial house in order, after getting divorced and remarrying. It wasn't her first brush with borrowing woes: Ms. Flores declared bankruptcy in 2005 after amassing about $500,000 in debt. She felt entitled so she hired her own personal chef, housekeeper, and took multiple trips to Hawaii.

You might be reading this story, thinking how ridiculous this lady is, but how about yourself? Are you saving at least 15 percent of your income, how does your retirement savings look, how about your debt? Forming good financial habits lasts a lifetime. The majority of people spend to not only satisfy a material need but more importantly, an emotional need. Psychologists say many people overspend to either fit in with peers or because of low self-esteem issues. Whatever your reason, let's break the cycle.

Here are some tips on how to do it:

- Unsubscribe to some of those shopping emails that cause you to impulse spend. Although I love to see the latest fashion designs, these companies are trying to entice you to buy something even if you don't need it! How many times do you see something you *must* have from a fashion email? Unsubscribe! You can always shop when you have the money and a purpose.

- Save before you spend. Do this with every paycheck, even if it's just a little. Make sure you've met your savings goals and reward yourself with something that doesn't cause additional debt.

- Take a look at your utilities: phone, cable, and internet. See if these companies offer new plans. It might be a pain to make the calls, but well worth the possible savings. Then use the savings to pay off debt or increase savings.

- Everyone by now has a wide variety of streaming services. Check your credit card/bank statements. You might be surprised to see how many of these you pay for every month: Netflix, Amazon Prime, HBO, music services, and others. Get rid of the ones you're not using any more. Once again, use the savings to pay off debt or increase savings.

- Do you eat out every night? How about breakfast and lunch? Restaurants can be very expensive. Allocate a certain amount of money you want to spend on food every week, including the grocery store and restaurants. People tend to overspend in both places. I'm not necessarily a foodie; however, do I really need fourteen pairs of shoes to go with my Little Black Dress? "Need" can be such a subjective word!

Be creative, you can do this!

You know yourself better than anyone; you know where the fat is.

CHAPTER 3
KNOW YOUR NUMBERS!

You don't have to be a geeky numbers person, but knowing your numbers is essential to just about everything. I can't stress this enough! How can you determine where to cut your spending and save more if you don't know where you're spending your money? When you go on a diet, are you incredibly vague about it? "I'm going to lose some weight." How much weight? How long will it take you? How are you going to do it? Reduce calories? How many? Reduce fat? How much? You get the picture. Knowing your numbers is essential to all stages of investing. How much do you make? How much do you spend? How much do you save? How much do you want to have by retirement?

When you're first getting started, you need everything. Saving money seems monumental but saving during this time is key to not piling on an enormous amount of debt because you want everything and you want it now. Of course, if you don't have the money for everything that you need immediately, you use credit cards as we talked about in the spending chapter. Before you know it, you've maxed out all the credit cards and you're saddled with college loan debt and the "need everything now" debt. That's trouble! It's hard to believe, but some of those "need now" items can wait even just a couple of months. Once you get a job and start earning money, give yourself a couple of months for an adjustment then start looking at your numbers. How much do you make? Do you have any existing debt? What are your expenses? Knowing your numbers really applies to everyone, not just people starting out in life. Everyone should know her numbers!

Set up a basic budget spreadsheet for monthly expenses. I use Excel but there are a ton of templates on the internet that make it easy. There are even some budgeting Apps, like Qapital or Digit, that you can use to make it easier. Later on, when you make more and have more expenses (that's how it works!), then you can expand your spreadsheet to every month of the year. That allows you to account for the months you have an additional expense like Christmas or car insurance that you only pay twice a year, and so on.

Also, if you're really having a hard time saving and finding some extra money to put away, shorten the timeframe for your goals. In other words, instead of budgeting monthly, figure out how much you can/can't spend weekly. If you decide you have $250 to spend every week, including groceries and entertainment, you'll be more careful about your purchases. You can even take out $250 in cash every week, so you see each dollar you spend. Watching dollar bills being spent is by far more painful than swiping a card.

Start out with something very basic like this, which is based off a person who makes $50,000 and is in the 25% tax bracket:

Household Expenses	
Rent	$900.00
Utilities	$150.00
Cable/Internet	$75.00
Cell Phone	$75.00
Food	$400.00
Car Expenses	
Loan	$200.00
Insurance	$75.00
Gas/Maintenance	$100.00
Student Loans	
Loan 1	$150.00
Loan 2	$175.00
Personal Care	
Hair/Beauty	$50.00
Entertainment	$250.00
Clothes	$200.00
Fitness/Yoga	$100.00
Prescriptions/Medical	$100.00
TOTAL	**$3,000.00**
Take Home Pay	$3,125.00
SAVINGS	**$125.00**

Once you know what your numbers are, set up your automatic savings plan. In this case, this person can save $62.50 each paycheck every month. It doesn't matter if it's only $20: Save what you can and increase it every time you get a raise or a bonus.

CHAPTER 4
WHAT'S YOUR STYLE?

When you look for clothes, what's your style? A little black dress, of course! You know what you like and sometimes you even have a special occasion that's not your everyday outfit, like a wedding. When you're looking for shoes, what are you looking for? Do you want exercise shoes, dress shoes, flats, boots, pumps, platforms? What's important to you? It is color, comfort, height of the heel, price, designer? Think the same way about choosing your investments.

Time frame and the goal for the money dictates quite a bit when it comes to what to do with your money. **I can't say it enough that the time frame for using the money is extremely important!** Equally important is your risk tolerance, even with money you don't need in the short term. If you work with a financial representative, you really need to know what that person is recommending, and it should fit you just like the sweater you bought. Your investments should suit your style. If you don't understand what your advisor is saying, don't hesitate to ask for clarification. That professional works for you, just like your hair stylist! There are some very important questions to ask yourself and make sure your financial representative knows:

- Time frame, time frame, time frame! How soon do I need to use this money? Short term (0-5 years), intermediate (5-10 years), or long term (10 years +).

- What's my goal; why am saving this money? House, college, retirement, shoes.

- What's most important to you? Is it growth, safety, income?

- How comfortable do you feel managing your own money? If the answer is *not at all*, then you should look for a money manager you can trust and one that doesn't charge a fortune. Most money managers charge around 1 percent.

A good rule of thumb is the shorter your time frame, the less risk you should take. In other words, if you need this money in the next year, you should keep your money in cash or low risk investments. The longer your time frame, ten years or more, the more risk you can take because you have time to smooth out the ups and downs of the stock market, so invest more in the stock market. In other words:

- 0-5 years = cash or very conservative (CDs or short-term bonds)

- 5-10 years = moderate (50-60% stocks and 40-50% bonds/cash)

- 10+ years = aggressive (At least 70% stocks)

Aside from knowing your goal and time frame, what type of investor are you? Some women wear a dress to everything while some wear jeans. Their clothes fit their personality/style. What's your investing personality? I gave you guidelines for how conservative/aggressive you should be according to your timeframe, but you can choose more or less risk. It's up to you; it's your money! Here's a chart that demonstrates conservative to aggressive "target asset mix" which just means how much or little you'd like to invest in the stock market.

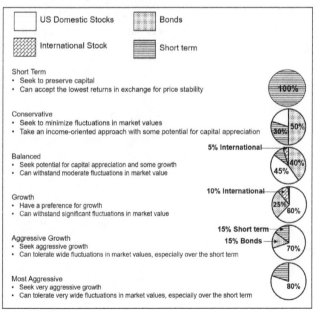

US Domestic Stocks
Bonds
International Stock
Short term

Short Term
- Seek to preserve capital
- Can accept the lowest returns in exchange for price stability

100%

Conservative
- Seek to minimize fluctuations in market values
- Take an income-oriented approach with some potential for capital appreciation

50%
30%

5% International

Balanced
- Seek potential for capital appreciation and some growth
- Can withstand moderate fluctuations in market value

40%
45%

10% International

Growth
- Have a preference for growth
- Can withstand significant fluctuations in market value

25%
60%

15% Short term
15% Bonds

Aggressive Growth
- Seek aggressive growth
- Can tolerate wide fluctuations in market values, especially over the short term

70%

Most Aggressive
- Seek very aggressive growth
- Can tolerate very wide fluctuations in market values, especially over the short term

80%

The two basic fundamentals of investing are asset allocation and diversification. I know that sounds complicated, but **asset allocation** just means you should have a certain amount of stocks, bonds (or fixed income) and cash, see the chart above!

Diversification just means you should have different types within each of those categories. For instance, instead of owning one type of company stock, you should own large, medium, and small companies as well as some international companies. Your bonds should include municipals, corporates, short term, intermediate term, and so on. Before you feel overwhelmed, there are many mutual funds that can do all of this for you. Balanced, asset allocation, growth and income, and target date funds all offer a diversified mix of stocks and bonds.

See, this is not so hard and there are many tools to help you! After all, everyone can use a curling iron, eyelash curler, or steamer to enhance your already beautiful self!

CHAPTER 5

ARE YOU SAVING LIKE A SISSY AND DO YOU HAVE A PLAN?

Now that we've stopped the overspending, let's talk about how much you save. Girls, are you hoping someone else will take care of you? Are you thinking you can just spend a ton then marry someone who did a good job saving? Is that why you're not saving? I've seen couples who don't want to get married because one of them has too much debt and the other partner doesn't want to assume debt they didn't accumulate. Don't count on anyone else; you never know what will happen. When it comes to saving, women get a bad name; however, it doesn't look like our country has a very high savings rate in general. Since 1960, the United States personal savings has ranged from under 10 percent to just over

13 percent. Out of the 195 countries listed currently in the world, the United States is generally ranked number 100 as far as our personal savings rate, although there are some countries with negative numbers. Ugh! We're definitely a consumer driven economy, meaning there's a ton of stuff available to buy and we buy it. Like so many things in life, it takes having a plan and discipline to reach your goal.

Retirement savings isn't much better. According to the Federal Reserve's "Report on the Economic Well-Being of U.S. Households in 2019," median retirement savings was $60,000 among all adults. That doesn't include employee sponsored savings accounts, like 401ks, or people with pensions. The vast majority of Americans don't feel they have enough saved for retirement. Keep in mind that if you're 64 years old with $219,000 saved, that means you can only live on $12,000 a year if you want the account to last through a typical retirement. Can you live on $12,000 a year? I don't know too many people who can. Even if you add $2,000 a month of social security, that's only $36,000 a year. What's the message? We all need to save more!

Let's put together a savings plan!

How much should I be saving is a question I was asked constantly. First of all, if you're saddled with debt, focus on paying that down to a manageable level before you work on building your savings. Secondly, there isn't a one size fits all answer to this question as everyone's time frame and lifestyle is different. I've seen people retire with millions and blow through all that money in a couple of years. It's unbelievable but it does happen. I've also seen people live happily on a rigid fixed income. How much you need all goes back to your personal style.

Normally, I tried to save 20 percent (this is a bit more aggressive than most can manage) of our household income and this is how I would divide it:

- Retirement Accounts: 10%

- College Savings: 4%

- General Investing Accounts: 5%

- Rainy Day – All Cash Account: 1%

Once we started making more, we saved more. When our kids graduated college, we were able to save more. Obviously, if you don't have children or they're already graduated then you don't need college savings. If you're saving for a large one-time expense, like a house, you might be saving more in general savings temporarily until you purchase the home. Make this your own personal savings plans, just like your own personal diet plan that works for you! If you're having problems achieving this level of savings, here's some ideas to help make it easier—if that's possible!

- Pay yourself first. Automate your savings so you have some money going into retirement accounts (401k, Roth IRA, Tra-ditional IRA, and so on) and some going into general savings. When you set up automatic savings, you don't count on having that money. Save a minimum 5 percent.

- If your company matches your contributions in a 401k, at least contribute the amount they match. Otherwise, you're not taking advantage of free money.

- If you need to put purchases on a credit card every month, cut back on your spending (see the Spending, Spending, Spending chapter). I know this is hard but take an honest look of what you're buying. Try to cut back things that don't matter as much. Are you eating out every day for lunch or dinner? Everyone has some padding, something they can give up without making a huge dent in their lifestyle.

- Every time you get a raise, increase your savings. I know it's hard, but you can do it. Chances are, you can increase your savings and still have a bit more to spend.

Save Your Money! You'll Be Glad You Did!

CHAPTER 6
LET'S GET STARTED WITH BASIC INVESTMENTS

Knowing Basic Types of Investments is Like Knowing the Difference Between Lipstick and Foundation! Now that we have our shoe fetish under control and our savings plan in place, let's start learning about investments. What's the matter, that doesn't sound fun? It would be easy to entice you with materialistic ideas: a red convertible Alfa Romeo, shopping in Milan, or converting a bedroom into a closet for all your clothes and shoes. However, the real benefit to saving and being disciplined with your money is independence. You have the power to control what happens to you; you're not at the mercy of someone else's decisions.

Let's review the basic types of investments:

Money Markets/Savings Accounts

These types of accounts just pay interest on your cash. Lately, they hardly pay any interest, but your cash is liquid if you need to use it. This is where most people keep their rainy-day funds.

CDs

CD stands for certificate of deposit. You can buy these at banks and brokerage firms. You invest a certain amount of money for a particular time frame, and they pay you interest. CDs can have short time frames, such as three months, a year, or several years. These are considered very conservative investments, so they don't pay very much. They are all FDIC (federally) insured up to $250,000 so even if the issuer goes out of business, you'll be able to get your money back.

Bonds

Bonds are basically loans that you make to corporations or governments. You earn interest while you are giving them the cash they need. This loan is only for a fixed period of time – 3 years, 5 years, 10 years, and so on. When the time has ended, you get your original investment back plus you get to keep the interest you've earned all along.

For example, let's say Coach Inc. sells five-year corporate bonds that pay a 3 percent yield. You buy a $10,000 Coach bond. Every year, you receive 3 percent interest until the end of five years. At that point, you get your $10,000 back. Bonds can pay their interest monthly, quarterly, semiannually, or annually.

Typically, bonds are considered a more conservative investment since you wouldn't normally lose the amount you originally invested. Most people either buy an individual bond and hold the bond until maturity, or they will buy a bond mutual fund that they can sell whenever they want. Don't get me wrong: Companies can go out of business and governments can go bankrupt, so some individual bonds can default but it's just not as common.

Many people in retirement like to have bond portfolios to live off the interest they receive. The investment is considered more conservative than many others and they can use the interest they receive like income. Many people also have a portion of their portfolio in bonds to offset the ups and downs of the stock market.

Mutual Funds

Mutual funds are incredibly popular because they're a whole group of investments all combined together into one fund. They help reduce the risk of buying just one company. Mutual funds are like a shell. They can be a group of stocks, a group of bonds, or even a combination of both, all bundled into one mutual fund. They can be very general and hold a group of large US companies or they can be very specific and hold only Biotech companies.

Let's say one person bought $10,000 of Procter & Gamble (P&G) stock and another person bought $10,000 of a mutual fund that holds P&G along with several other large companies. All of a sudden, P&G has a problem with their Tide pods and people stop buying them so, of course, their stock drops.

The person who owns the P&G stock now only has $9,000 because their stock dropped 10 percent. However, the person who bought the mutual fund has $9,800 because P&G was only one of many companies in the fund and its drop didn't have that big of an impact on the overall mutual fund. I'm just making up numbers to prove a point, but you can see how mutual funds sometimes can help mitigate risk.

By the way, it works just the opposite when the stock goes way up! One other important fact about mutual funds is that they only trade once a day, at the end of the day. You cannot pick the price you want to buy or sell a mutual fund like you can a stock. When you buy or sell a mutual fund, you get the price at the end of the day, whatever it is.

Stocks

When you own even one share of stock, you own part of a publicly traded company. Let's say you buy a share of Coach. You now own part of the Coach Inc. and maybe some of their handbags! Most of the time, you buy shares of a stock because you believe the company has good growth potential. Let's pretend Coach sold for $10 a share when you bought it. They come out with a spectacular handbag design, everyone buys them, their profits soar, and as a result, their stock now sells for $15 a share. You just made $5 for every share you own.

Typically, buying one individual stock is riskier. You're depending on one single company to do well, grow, and not have any missteps. In other words, it's like saying "Coach will always have to have better handbags than Louis Vuitton" (that's probably not going to happen!). However, buying single stocks can make you earn more than anything else because a company can have explosive growth.

Stocks trade all day long on the various stock exchanges. When you buy/sell a stock, you can either buy/sell it at whatever the price is right now, or you can choose the price you want. When you choose a price, there's no guarantee that you will get that price but it is nice to have the option.

ETFs

ETF stands for Exchange Traded Funds. These are also mutual funds because they hold a group of investments in each fund. The *huge* difference between ETFs and Mutual Funds is that you can trade an ETF just like a stock. That way you get the best of both worlds. You can try to reduce the risk of owning one single company but now you can trade it whenever you want and you can even set a price, just like a stock.

CHAPTER 7
Account Types
Where Do I Put These Investments?

Not all closets are created equal; after all, would you put your shoes in your food pantry? Closets are a place where you can store anything: shoes (of course), sweaters, dresses, luggage, Christmas decorations, food—you get the idea. However, you want to make sure you store the right things in the right closet. Think of accounts the same way. An investment account can hold many different types of investments like stocks, mutual funds, bonds, ETFs, cash, or CDs, but they are not taxed the same way and some accounts have age or investment restrictions. For example, a savings account only holds cash. A retirement account can't be used until age 59 ½ without penalty. A general brokerage account gets taxed every year. The point is that different types of accounts serve different purposes.

Many people confuse account types with investments. For instance, I've heard people say, "I invest. I have a Roth IRA." A Roth IRA is a type of retirement account but what's in that Roth? Does it hold stocks, mutual funds, cash, ETFs? Those are the actual investments. Let's review a few types of accounts and how they're taxed (this is really why you have different types of accounts).

Bank Savings Account

This is a very limited account where you only earn interest on cash and you are taxed every year on the interest you received during the year. You cannot buy any other type of investment in this account.

General Investing Account/Brokerage Account

This is like a huge walk-in closet. You can open these accounts (sometimes called brokerage accounts) at an investment firm, like Fidelity Investments (not that I'm biased), Charles Schwab, Merrill Lynch, Edward Jones, and others. Sometimes banks offer investment accounts as well, although I'm not a big fan of banks. You are taxed on everything that happens in this account during the year. If your stock, mutual fund, or ETF pays a dividend, you'll be taxed on it like its income for that year. If you sell a stock, mutual fund, or ETF and you have a gain (congratulations!), you'll be taxed on it for that year's taxes. *Nothing* is deferred like retirement accounts. You can use this account for any type of savings, cars, sofa, LBD, shoes, house, and so on. Although you can use these at any time, including retirement, it's *not* specifically a retirement account.

Roth IRA

This *is* a retirement account! If you qualify for a Roth, this account is a fantastic way to save for retirement. Roth IRAs have annual income restrictions, so not everyone qualifies for a Roth. You can put $6,000 per year into this account, plus another $1000 if you are 50 years old and older. We will cover retirement accounts in the next section, so don't worry if you don't understand the specific retirement accounts just yet—you will! You can put almost any type of investment in this account (stocks, mutual funds, CDs, bonds, blah, blah, blah). You put money that's already been taxed into this account and *never* pay taxes on the growth as long as you keep the growth in the account until you are at least 59 ½ years old.

Traditional IRA

This *is* a retirement account, too! It does *not* have an annual income restriction but you can only put $6,000/year into this account as well, plus another $1000 if you are 50 years old and older. You will get a tax credit for money you put into this account so that means the money you put in is not taxed for that particular year. You will; however, pay taxes on everything that comes out of this account (wait until at least 59 ½ to take anything out).

401k/403b

These accounts are also retirement accounts, but they are only available through your employer. You can contribute $19,500 annually and an additional $6,500 if you're over the age of 50. Your employer can deduct money right out of your paycheck to put into these accounts, plus many times the employer will also match what you contribute. If your employer matches, count your blessings! This is free retirement money and who doesn't want that?! Make sure you contribute at least the amount they match.

Normally, this money is pre-tax money so just like a Traditional IRA, it means the money you put in is not taxed for that particular year and it helps reduce your taxable income. However, many 401k accounts now also offer a Roth option, which is fantastic if you qualify for a Roth. Many times, you can contribute to both options. If you need a tax break for the current year, use the Traditional option. If you don't and you qualify, use the Roth.

Now we know where we can store our investments, we can talk about strategy. This might not sound as fun as the strategy to attract that really good-looking guy you've had your eye on, but the money you save will probably last a lot longer than your interest in him!

CHAPTER 8
ᕼOW TO ᕼET ᏚTARTED

Okay, so you know your numbers, so check off the basics:

- ☑ budget
- ☑ savings plan
- ☑ spending's under control
- ☑ know basic investments
- ☑ know basic account types.

And then you ask yourself: Now how do I actually get started?! Here are several important things you can do to get the ball rolling. Not all of these apply to everyone, so pick what is most applicable to your situation.

Get Started!

- Make sure you have the accounts open that you need: savings account, general brokerage account, retirement account.

- A bank savings account or the cash account of your general brokerage account is the best place for your savings account (rainy day fund). It's just cash!

- As I said previously, a brokerage firm, like Fidelity Investments, Charles Schwab, or another reputable firm is the best place for your general brokerage account. Go online or call the company's customer service number and ask them to help you open the account if you don't feel comfortable doing it by yourself. You can always find a local representative if you prefer to open the account in person.

- Direct your money according to your savings plan! What percentage goes into savings, the brokerage account, and your retirement account?

- If your company offers a 401k or 403b (these are retirement accounts), make sure you contribute. If your company offers matching, contribute at least the amount they match.

- If your company doesn't offer a retirement plan, open a Traditional or Roth IRA at the same brokerage firm that holds your general brokerage account.

Automate Your Savings

- If your paycheck is deposited into a checking account, transfer a small amount for your rainy-day fund.

- Link your checking account at the bank with your general brokerage account and set up an automatic investment transfer. Let's say every time you get paid, you transfer $200 into your general investing account. Then you can make sure that money goes into the specific investment you'd like every month. You won't even miss the money after a while. Ask how to set this up!

- Your 401k or 403b is taken out of every paycheck so that's already automated. If you have your own Traditional or Roth IRA, you can automate your contributions into these accounts from your general brokerage account or from your checking account. Once again, ask how to set this up!

Automating your savings means that you're "dollar cost averaging." Sounds like a fancy term. All it means is when you're buying a little bit at a time, all the time so sometimes you buy when the market is up, sometimes it's pretty flat, and sometimes it's down. Your investments over time will average all those purchases. It's a great way to stick to a plan and build wealth.

Most of the people I know who became wealthy did it by saving all the time, even if it's just a little bit. They didn't get rich quick by cashing in on some penny stock that hit the big time! It takes discipline and a plan! Just like your diet. Haven't you ever seen people who lose a ton of weight at once with some diet scheme only to gain it back a short time later?! No one says, I'm just going to lose weight. Well, how much weight, by what time, and how are you going to do it? You've got to have a plan that allows you to lose a reasonable amount of weight over time!

CHAPTER 9
WHY IT'S OKAY TO TAKE SOME RISK

Is it risky to wear leopard print shoes with a red dress? Not according to my daughter! However, you might feel safer with a black pair. Maybe a black dress with those black shoes—even safer! That's basically how most women invest. They're so afraid of losing money; so afraid of a drop in the market that they shy away from it. What if I invest in a stock and it goes down? I could have stayed in cash and not lost anything. Believe it or not, that fear costs women money. A *Wall Street Journal* article by Carol Ryan, "Women Investors Are Bucking Stocks" discusses why women won't embrace stocks and how it's a problem for them and the market. I couldn't agree more. Before we start building portfolios and picking investments, let's talk about the stock market and why it's not as scary as you think.

It's really not surprising that men are more comfortable with the market considering most fathers talk to their sons about investing and most investment companies' market to men. Men in general are more comfortable taking financial risk. (Of course, women take the biggest risk of all: bearing children.) There are the typical reasons why women pull back from financial discussions: Obtuse jargon, too many investment choices and just some general confusion with the whole process. Even when women do invest, they typically like bonds, real estate, and cash. How does that hurt women? The stock market over time returns an average of 10 percent with some years considerably higher. Fixed income products and money markets right now don't even get close to 1 percent.

You'd have to invest in a 10-year US treasury bond to maybe get 1.5 percent interest. Such conservative investing generally doesn't keep up with the rate of inflation, meaning you're actually losing money even though the balance isn't changing. When the price of everything around you is going up but your pool of money stays the same, it's essentially shrinking. You need some growth! Aside from that, it's important to make your money work for you.

Don't get me wrong, just as we discussed previously, it's important to have some cash, a rainy-day cash fund of three to six months of essential expenses. And of course, time frame matters with your investments. If you need the money in a short amount of time, don't put it in the market. If you have a moderate amount of time, invest moderately by taking risk with maybe half of the amount. If you have a long period of time, more than 10 years, you can afford to take some risk since you have time to smooth out the ups and downs of the market.

There are several ways to reduce the risk of the market. Afterall, not all stocks/companies are the same. Think about your shoe closet. You might have 5" heels for a fun night out, 3" work shoes that aren't necessarily fun but they're comfortable, professional and do the trick all day. Flats for something a bit dressier than tennis shoes. Even my tennis shoes have different purposes: running, tennis, dressy casual. This is the same reason you hear different categories of stocks such as growth, value, or dividend just to name a few. One of the best ways to reduce risk is to make sure you diversify what you own. Don't put all of your money into one stock and then bite your newly manicured nails all day watching what it does. Mutual funds and ETFs are a great way to buy into a grouping of investments instead of just one. This mitigates risk.

It can be risky to wear 5-inch high heels, especially with that short red dress! You might sprain your ankle, trip, or attract a guy obsessed with red stilettos. Heaven forbid you marry him! Investing in an up-and-coming biotech pharmaceutical company is not the same as investing in a steady as she goes utility company that pays a dividend. There are several thousand stocks from which to choose. Typically, large established companies are less volatile than small companies trying to survive. The S&P 500 is an index made up of 500 of the largest companies in the United States. Many other investments are compared to this index for that very reason.

Another way to limit risk is to invest a little on a regular basis. We talked about this in the Getting Started chapter. This is called dollar cost averaging. All it means is sometimes you're buying when the market is high, sometimes it's low, and sometimes it's in between so it all averages out in the end. It's very easy to set up an automatic investing plan with most firms, especially when you're buying into a mutual fund. This takes some of the scariness out of the ups and downs of the market because you're buying in all the time (maybe monthly or bi-monthly) so you're counting on everything averaging out.

As you can see, the market isn't just made up of 5-inch heeled stocks! It's possible to buy less volatile stocks, diversify what you own, and average out your purchases so it doesn't seem so you can breathe easier. No risk, no reward is absolutely true when it comes to investing but that doesn't mean you have to take the highest possible risk. Maybe you can start out with some red flats then work your way up to a comfortable professional shoe before you dabble in those 5-inch heels!

CHAPTER 10
How to Build
a Basic Portfolio

Now that we've decided it's okay to take some risk, let's talk about how to build a portfolio. Keep in mind that I'm generalizing and giving examples of some ways to put together a group of investments, so you have a starting point. There are so many different philosophies and risk levels that it would be impossible to demonstrate all the possibilities. Per our previous conversation, we're going to build three portfolios based on shoe height! We'll have a relatively conservative flat shoe type of portfolio, then a moderate professional heel level of risk, and finally a night out on the town 5" leopard print pump.

No matter what the risk level, I always anchor an account with a broad-based index or balanced fund, depending on the time frame and risk level. Examples of a broad-based index fund would be the S&P 500 Index or the Total Market Index. Both of these offer a huge number of stocks all in one fund, which means you're diversified with one holding. If there's a shorter time frame or lower risk tolerance, I'll use a balanced fund such as Fidelity's Balance Fund (FBALX). These types of funds combine lower risk investments like CDs and bonds together with stocks. They're like a one stop shop!

Once the account is anchored, then I will add investments to either lower the risk level or try to get a bump over and above the market. Keep in mind that these are purely examples and certainly not the only way to build a portfolio. While I'm using mutual funds in these examples, many times you can also use ETFs (see previous chapter for definition).

Conservative Flat Shoe Portfolio

- Cash 10%

- Short Term Bond Index Fund 10%

- Balanced Fund 50%

- Strategic Dividend & Income Fund 15%

- Select Utilities Fund 15%

Moderate Professional Heel Portfolio

- Cash 10%

- Short Term Bond Index Fund 10%

- Balanced Fund 50%

- Large Cap Value Fund 20%

- Consumer Staples Sector Fund 10%

High Risk 5" Pumps Portfolio

- Cash 5%
- S&P 500 Index Fund 40%
- Health Care Sector Fund 10%
- Consumer Discretionary Sector Fund 10%
- Biotech Stock 10%
- Energy Stocks 10%
- Technology Stocks 15%

Truthfully, the High Risk 5-inch Pumps Portfolio is more my style and fun to put together, but that's definitely not for everyone. Don't feel bad if your comfort level is much more conservative. If you have a shorter time frame, that portfolio would be more appropriate. As your account grows, be mindful of the percentages. If we're having a good year and all of a sudden, your balanced fund or large cap fund is a much higher percentage of your portfolio, you're now taking on more risk than you'd like. A good idea is to skim a little off these funds and keep the proceeds in cash or put them in the short-term bond index fund. This is called rebalancing and helps to keep you at an appropriate level of risk.

CHAPTER 11
I Want to Learn About Stocks

Let's say you've become comfortable with your savings plan, the types of accounts and the types of investments. Yay! You've already achieved success! Now you want to learn how to pick and trade individual stocks. There are so many stocks! Not all stocks are the same, either. There are slow growing utility stocks that pay a dividend, there are fast growing tech companies who don't pay any dividend, there are large, medium, and small companies, and so on. How do you know which one to pick? What in the world is a dividend? How do you know who to believe? Trust me, when you start asking around about stocks, everyone will have an opinion and some people will even offer a "sure thing" to buy.

Before we get started picking, let's make sure you understand the components of a stock. Sorry if this seems elementary, but I want to make sure you understand the basics first. Of course, buying stock means you're buying a piece of ownership in a publicly traded company. Wouldn't it be great to tell your friends that you own part of the Moet Hennessy Louis Vuitton company?! Champagne and handbags, what more do you need?! I'd be equally happy if I could pronounce it correctly! Every publicly traded company has a trading symbol. For instance, Moet Hennessy Louis Vuitton's trading symbol is LVMUY. Google is GOOG, Ford is F, Procter & Gamble is PG, and so on. When you place your stock trade, you'll use the company's trading symbol.

Stocks trade all day, so their price goes up and down all the time. Regular market hours are 9:30 – 4:00 pm EST and what-ever the stock is trading at during those hours is called the Market price. When you look at a stock quote during the day, you'll see the Market price as well as a Bid and Ask price. If you're buying a stock, you'll get the Ask price (this is a market order – we'll talk about order types later). If you're selling your stock, you'll receive the Bid price. Don't let the terms confuse you. Just remember, you're buying someone else's shares and that's what they're Ask(ing) for it. You really only need to remember one side of the equation. If you remember that you're buying at the Ask price then obviously, you would be selling at the Bid price.

You'll also notice "volume" on a stock quote. That's just how many shares are trading that day. For most major companies, it's huge. For instance, Google trades well over a million shares a day. The only time I really worried about volume is if I was trading a "thinly traded" stock. Let's say your stock only trades a couple thousand shares during the day and you bought several hundred. Your order would be a big percentage of that day's trading volume and could really affect the price of that stock. If you're just getting started, you probably don't need to worry about this.

You'll also see the dividend yield on a stock quote. Since I've mentioned them so many times, let's talk about dividends. What is a dividend?! A dividend is like the interest a stock pays you that has nothing to do with its price. Typically, after a company sees how much their quarterly earnings are, they decide if they're going to pay their shareholders a dividend and if so, how much. Dividends are a very important part of investing. Let's say you're retired and you want to be more conservative with your money, but you still want to make some type of income. Some people buy low volatility stocks, like utilities (gas & electric companies), that pay a good dividend. That way they don't need to worry too much about the money they invest and they get some good income as well. For many mature companies that are done with explosive growth, this is a good way to attract investors. It's also not a bad strategy when the stock market is high and you're worried about stocks being overpriced; many people look for good dividend paying stocks. There are a couple of terms you need to know when it comes to dividends that are important:

- **Record Date**: This just means that all shareholders on record as of this date will receive the dividend. That means you own the stock on that date. It's important because some people buy or sell in between the record and pay date, so they're not sure if they get the dividend.

- **Ex Date**: This is the first day the stock trades without the buy-er getting the dividend. If you buy on the Ex Date, don't expect to get that quarterly dividend.

- **Pay Date**: This is self-explanatory, but this is the day you receive the dividend. It can be up to a month after the Record Date.

An example of what a stock quote looks like is in living color on my website, carenlaverty.com.

Now that you know the basics (don't be surprised if you have to look back over some terms occasionally), let's look at some fundamental things to know when picking a stock.

First of all, before you listen to anyone else, believe it or not, you need to know why you're buying this stock. Are you looking for long term growth, dividends/income producing stocks, or a short-term money maker? One of the biggest mistakes I see people make, is buying stocks without knowing why, doing their own research, or considering the growth of the company. Make sure the stock your picking matches the reason for buying the stock. In other words, if you're looking for a stock that pays a big dividend, don't buy a speculative high growth tech stock with no dividend just because it sounds cool. Stick to your goal.

1. Know what the company does! This sounds so simple, but I can't tell you how many people buy a stock because someone else told them about it or they saw in the news without doing any of their own research.

2. If you're buying a stock for long term growth, you should know how much of a

dividend they pay. Remember, a dividend is like the interest you're paid on the stock that has nothing to do with the price.

3. If you're familiar with stocks at all, you've probably heard of a P/E (Price to Earnings) Ratio. This gauges how the company's stock is valued; is it overvalued or undervalued. Let's say a stock has a P/E ratio of $15. That means you're willing to pay $15 for every $1 per earnings. While a lower P/E ratio is usually better, that's not usually the case with new and fast-growing companies. It's certainly one thing to consider, but don't buy based on P/E ratio alone.

4. Is the company profitable? Does it make money and how does it compare to its competitors? Don't feel like you need to whip out your old college accounting book but look at their earnings to make sure they make money. This is once again tricky with new companies. Some of the biggest tech companies weren't profit-able for years.

5. Look at the company's stock price chart. Try to see patterns with their price. You obviously want to buy low and sell high (buy at a low stock price and then sell when it gets higher), but you don't want to buy a stock that looks like it's perpetually sad. If it looks like it's been treading water or even tumbling down for a while, you might want to look for something else.

6.   Growth!!! How does the company plan to grow?! If you're not buying a company that plans to grow, then it better have a pretty nice dividend. When Facebook first went public, its share price went down for a while because people couldn't figure out how a social media company could make money. To their credit, they came out with an advertising plan and have done tremendous.

These are just some things to consider when buying a stock. Stocks are fun to research and trade (I know fun might be a relative term here, but I find it fun!); however, I do want to caution you a bit. When you own a stock, you own one company, so your investment is entirely dependent on how that one company is doing. Let's say you bought a bank stock and for the most part all the bank stocks were having a fantastic year. Suddenly, you find out that your bank opened up tons of phony accounts illegally – this actually happened. Now your stock is plummeting and you're panicking! Ugh! You thought banks were doing good, you thought this bank was good, you thought you would make money – not lose it! Just remember, if you're new to buying stocks, make sure you've got your bases covered with a diversified portfolio and you're okay risking the money you're investing. There's *always* the risk of losing all of the money you use to buy an individual stock.

CHAPTER 12
HOW DO I TRADE STOCK?
STOCKS ARE LIKE MEAN GIRLFRIENDS!
PROTECT YOURSELF!

Now that you've picked your stock, you need to know how to trade stock. Have you ever gotten together with a mean girlfriend? She's the type of girl you're not sure why you're still friends with her. There's always the possibility of a put down or snide remark so you constantly feel defensive like you have to have your guard up all the time. Think of trading stock the same way. Your stocks are mean girlfriends; you never know when they're going to take a huge dip resulting in a loss of money and stock picking confidence. Both scenarios make you feel like crud. Not sure what you should do with your snippy friend, but I can help you protect yourself when you buy a stock.

There are different types of trades you can place when you buy/sell a stock and there are different types of protectionary orders as well. Let's start out with the two most common ways to buy and sell stock.

- **Market Order**: Stock prices go up and down all day. When you buy your stock at the market, your order will fill at the very next available price no matter what it is. This type of or-der is only good for that day and will probably fill immediately.

- **Limit Order**: If you want to buy your stock at a price lower than its current price, that's called a limit order. Let's say Sugarplum Shoe Company is trading at $20/share but you don't want to buy it until it drops to $18. You can place an order to buy at a limit price of $18. This order can either be good for just that day or good-'til-cancelled (GTC) which stays open for anywhere from 30 to 180 days, depending on where you trade. Of course, if the stock price falls to your price or better, the order will fill in less time. (This also applies if you want to sell your stock above the current market price.)

So now you own your mean girlfriend stock. What will she do to you? Will she be in a good mood for once and go up or will she be her typical mean self and tumble down? Protect yourself. Here are some orders that protect you from losing too much.

- **Stop Loss**: This order has one trigger then turns into a market order. If you buy a stock at $20 a share and don't want to hold it if it tumbles down to $15. Your stop loss order will trigger at $15 or lower and become a market order so you have less control over the price, but the order is easier to fill.

- **Stop Limit**: This order has two triggers. Using the previous example, if your stock falls to $15, this order becomes a limit order and will not fill unless the stock hits $15 or better again. These orders don't work as well if your stock is just plummeting downward. In other words, you have more control over the price but they're harder to fill.

- **Trailing Stop Loss**: Trailing orders follow your stock as it goes up but not when it goes down. You can set these up by a% or by a $ amount. If you buy a stock at $20 and your stock goes up to $25, you might not want to keep your stop loss order at $15 so you place a trailing stop loss order at $5 increments. That way, when your stock goes to $25, your trailing stop loss will adjust to $20 instead of $15 (you can also do this with a certain % as well). As with a regular stop loss order, there's still only one trigger then it becomes a market order.

- **Trailing Stop Limit**: This is the same exact concept as above but using a limit order to trail the stock. Remember, that means your stock has two triggers which give you more control over the price but becomes harder to fill.

Please use caution with trailing orders. Sometimes the market has a very volatile day and if your order is too close to the actual stock price, your order might fill just because of the one-day volatility.

Here's a chart to demonstrate the order types:

	Buy	Sell
Market Price	Stop Loss Stop Limit Trailing Stop Loss Trailing Stop Limit	Limit
	Limit	Stop Loss Stop Limit Trailing Stop Loss Trailing Stop Limit

Remember, "Market Price" is just the current trading price of your stock.

- Orders above the market price are higher than the current price.

- Orders below the market price are lower than the current price.

- Let's use the example of a stock that trades for $50/share:

- If I want to buy the stock at whatever it's trading at now ($50/share), that's a **Market Order**.

- If I want to buy the stock lower than what it's trading at, then I can place a **Limit Order** lower than $50/share, $45 for example.

If I own the stock and I want to sell it for more than the current price, then I place a Sell Limit Order for above the Market Price, $55 as an example.

If I own the stock but I want to protect myself from this stock tumbling, I'll place a Stop Loss, Stop Limit, Trailing Stop Loss, or Trailing Stop Limit at $40 for example. (Stop Loss is the most common type of protectionary order because it's the easiest to fill, although your price is not guaranteed)

CHAPTER 13
WHAT ARE OPTIONS?

What in the world is an option? When I look in my shoe closet there are several options! #shoefettish Obviously we're not talking about trading shoes and although shoe choices can very well be confusing, they're not nearly as confusing as learning about options. There are suddenly many young adults trading options on platforms such as Robinhood. Trading options can be riskier but also much less expensive than buying a stock, which is why so many young people are attracted to them. Of course, there are several reasons and strategies for trading options, so let's learn the basics together.

First of all, **an option is a contract** attached to a stock; it's not the actual stock. It says you are either going to buy or sell that stock at a particular price by a particular expiration date. People use options for many reasons. Sometimes, they want to lock in a gain they have on a stock, sometimes they want to generate some income by selling options, or they might want to speculate about the direction of a stock. Options have their own terminology that makes them sound more confusing that they are.

The two main types of options are **calls and puts**. Here's the direction you would like the underlying stock to go if you buy or sell a call or put:

- Buy a Call contract = you think the stock will go up

- Sell (also called **Writing**) a Call contract = you think the stock will go down

- Buy a Put contract = you think the stock will go down

- Sell (also called **Writing**) a Put contract = you think the stock will go up

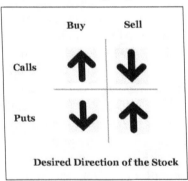

Secondly, each option contract represents **100 shares** of the underlying stock. The price associated with the option is called the **strike price**. That's just the price at which you'd like to either buy or sell the underlying stock. When you buy an option, you pay what's called a **premium**. That's just the price of the option contract. When you sell an option, you receive a premium. That's what someone paid you for this options contract. Most option contracts expire worthless; however, if a contract is used for the intended purpose, it's called **exercised**.

Finally, if you own the stock associated with an option contract you sold, it is call **covered**. If you don't own the underlying stock, the option you sold is either **cash covered** or **uncovered**. Selling an uncovered option can be very risky, so we're not going to bother talking any more about that!

Now that you're thoroughly confused with the terminology, let's go through a couple of examples of how people use options:

1. Let's say I bought 100 shares of Little Black Dress Company (LBDC) at $20 a share. Now I can sell (write) a covered call with a strike price of $30. Here's what happens: I receive a premium because someone bought this option and it's a covered option because I own the shares. If the stock reaches $30/share and my option is exercised, I have to sell them my shares of LBDC at $30/share. **Summary:** I received money from the premium and even though I had to sell my shares, I locked in a profit of $10/share. This is called a **Covered Call**.

2. LBDC is now trading at $25/share but I don't want to buy 100 shares of them until they go back down to $20/share. I have the cash to pay for this trade but I'm just waiting

for the shares to drop in price. Instead of just waiting, I can sell (write) one put contract with a strike price of $20. **Summary:** I receive money from the premium while I'm waiting for the price to drop. When it does, I'll buy the stock at a price I chose (the strike price). This is called writing a **Cash Covered Put.**

3. I would like to buy 300 shares of the LBDC that is now trading at $25/share but I'm not sure I really want to spend $7,500 on one stock. They have a fantastic new black dress that's in high demand! Instead of buying the shares, I'll buy 3 call options at a strike price of $28/share for $200 and wait to see if the stock goes up. If the stock goes up, the value of my option will go up as well. Let's say LBDC is now trading at $30/share. I can either sell my option for a profit or see if the option gets exercised. If it gets exercised, I will have to buy 300 shares at $28/share. I can either choose to sell these and make a profit or hold the shares to see if the stock goes up even higher. **Summary:** I don't have to spend a large amount of money to be in control of the same number of shares. If the LBDC stock doesn't go up and my option isn't "in the money", then the risk to me is that I lose the premium I paid for the option and it expires worthless. This sounds better than losing money on a stock and hoping it ends up going up in price again. This is called buying a bull **Call Option.**

In the last example, I used the term "**in the money**". If my stock is trading at \$25/share and I buy an option with a strike price at or below \$25/share, then it's considered in the money. That's because I would have the ability to buy the stock at the same or lower price that it's trading, which is a good thing! Same with the other way around, selling a stock at or above its current trading level.

Hope this helps make options a little less complicated. You might need to read the terminology over and over a couple of times before it makes sense. Don't worry if it takes a while. It will become even more clear when you place your first options trade!

CHAPTER 14
SECTORS OF THE ECONOMY

Have you ever divided up or arranged anything? Of course you have! Maybe you separate your summer sandals from your formal evening shoes or your everyday work shoes. I used to be able to separate my grey hair from my non-grey hair by pulling them out but that's not feasible anymore unless I'd like some pretty big bald spots! Or how about your groceries? You probably divide them up by breakfast, lunch, dinner, and so on. The various industries in our economy are so big and diverse that we can divide them up too to see which section of the economy is doing good or not so good.

I grew up in Warren, Ohio which is about an hour southeast of Cleveland, close to Youngstown. This entire area was incredibly dependent on the automobile industry. Warren had electrical wiring plants, Youngstown and Cleveland had steel plants, Akron had tire/rubber plants and Lordstown had assembly plants. You get the picture. In the 1970s, small Japanese cars were introduced into the American market and everyone bought them. The American cars were big, heavy, and not fuel efficient. Guess what happened? The American car companies struggled for years, so the Automotive Industry (in the Industrials Sector) of our economy was not very good in the 70s. Some of those areas never recovered and the sector itself took a long time to recover as well.

Now that you're thoroughly depressed and maybe wanting to buy an American made car, let me tell you the good news about investing in sectors. There are eleven different sectors and several industries within each sector.

- Consumer Discretionary

- Consumer Staples

- Energy

- Financial

- Healthcare

- Industrials

- Information Technology

- Materials

- Real Estate

- Telecommunication Services

- Utilities

For instance, the Consumer Staples sector includes six different industries: Beverages, Food & Staples Retailing, Food Products, House-hold Products, Personal Products, and Tobacco. These industries are considered necessary items in our economy so even if we're in a down-turn and people don't have a ton of extra money, they'll still need these staples. I don't know about you, but even if we're struggling and trying to pay bills, we still eat food. The difference is, when you're struggling, you eat at home. When you have extra money, you put on those fantastic new shoes and eat out at restaurants which would be industries included in the Consumer Discretionary sector. Get the picture?

The great thing about investing in just one sector of the economy is that it gives you a chance to gain more than the overall market without taking the risk of investing in just one company. As in our previous example, if the economy is not doing so well, maybe unemployment is high and our overall growth is low or even negative, so people are not going to have the money to spend on high priced items (like a new car or refrigerator). In that case, I would invest in a Consumer Staples fund or ETF since consumer staples represent the necessities of life in-stead of luxuries. On the other hand, if our economy has really strong growth and people have money to spare, I would invest in a Consumer Discretionary fund or ETF. For many years, as you can imagine, the Information Technology Sector was booming and so was Healthcare. The point is, it's sometimes easier to predict a particular sector of the economy in-stead of which particular company within those sectors will be the one worth taking a risk.

Investing in sectors goes hand in hand with business cycle investing. Our economy goes through recovery, expansion, and contraction. While this might sound confusing, it just means sometimes the economy is really growing, sometimes it's actually getting smaller, and sometimes it treads water with a recovery breather. As I was saying previously, certain sectors do better at different stages of the economy. If you're interested in sectors, it's worthwhile to know what stage of the economy we're in and which sectors do well in that stage. Since I'm trying to keep this book pretty fundamental, if you're interested in investing in sectors, do your research!

CHAPTER 15
WHY DOES EVERYONE MAKE SUCH A BIG DEAL ABOUT RETIREMENT?

Imagine what you do for a one-week vacation. You stop the mail and the newspaper, have someone take care of your pets, buy your plane tickets, make hotel reservations, plan activities and maybe even buy some tickets ahead of time. Naturally, you need to go shopping! Who wants to go to the beach in the same old bathing suit and of course that suit needs to match your beach bag, your flip flops, and cover up? Duh.

Now think of retirement as the longest vacation you'll ever take, except the income you use to pay for your vacation is gone—you're retired! So now you must rely on your savings, and if you're lucky, you have some retirement income (like a pension or social security).

What if you live 25-30 years in retirement? That's a pretty darn long vacation and you want to make sure you have the ability to enjoy it!

Let's put on our female planning hats.

There are many types of retirement plans, so what should you choose and how much should you contribute? The rule of thumb is:

- Max out your 401k/403b first - $19,500 annually and an extra $6,500 for people aged 50 and over.

- Then contribute to a Roth IRA if you qualify under the income limits. Single households can earn up to $124k and married filing joint can earn up to $196k for the full contribution amount of $6,000 ($7,000 for age 50 and over). There are phase out amounts for single households between $124-$139k and married filing joint between $196-$206.

- If you still have more to contribute, pat yourself on the back and make an after-tax contribution to a Traditional IRA. They have the same contribution limits as a Roth IRA, $6,000 ($7,000 for age 50 and over).

Important: If you're a spouse and don't work outside the home, you can still make a spousal contribution to a Roth or Traditional in these same amounts.

Don't be overwhelmed by the amounts. If you can't max out any of the accounts, do what you can every year with the goal of eventually maxing out the contribution amounts. After all, this is one vacation you don't want to end and don't want to return to work.

Just a piece of advice: DO NOT take money out of retirement accounts before your retirement. You will pay taxes and a penalty, plus you're taking money away from your retirement savings as well as the growth of your investments. **Do not** take out loans on your 401k especially if it suspends your contributions. Too many companies make it soooo easy to get a loan. The idea of a retirement savings account is to save.

How much do you need to retire? Everyone always asks how much they need to retire as if there's one simple number that applies to everyone. It's like the stretchy one size fits all pants. Do they really fit everyone? No. One of my relatives is over 300 pounds; I'm 110 pounds. Those pants are not fitting both of us – I don't care how stretchy they are! How much money you need in retirement depends on your lifestyle. You'll see guidelines say you need about 70 – 90 percent of your pre-retirement income to live comfortably; however, it really depends on your retirement plans. I've seen happily retired clients living off their social security and $500k in investments. I've also seen clients with millions of dollars blow throw all of that money within ten years.

One strategy we would use when helping clients plan for retirement is to make sure they had enough "certain and continuous" income (pensions, social security, annuities) to pay for essential expenses. Essential expenses include everything you need to live without any extras, meaning housing, food, utilities, etc. That way if the world goes crazy, they would always have enough to pay for their basic living expenses. Then we would use general investing and retirement accounts for all discretionary spending like vacations, new cars, LBD, and of course, new shoes (the fun stuff!).

Essential Expenses	**Discretionary Expenses**
- Mortgage/Rent	- Vacation to Italy
- Food	- Valentino Shoes
- Utilities	- Suede Coat

What if you don't have enough "certain and continuous" income? After all, not very many companies pay a pension anymore, so most people only have social security which is not usually enough to cover essential expenses. One solution is to take a portion of your assets and annuitize them to create your own pension. If you're not familiar with annuities, they're an insurance product where you put in a lump sum of money and the insurance company agrees to pay you a fixed amount of money every year for the rest of your life.

You want to make sure you know all your numbers before you decide how much to annuitize. The benefit of doing this is that you will extend the life of your assets for as long as you live. The downside is that you can't take out a lump sum of money in case you need a new furnace or car. That's why you want to make sure you still have enough liquid assets to cover unexpected and discretionary expenses. Also, be careful of hidden fees with annuities. I own two annuities and neither of them have expenses over 1%. Old fashion annuities were notorious for having a massive amount of fees.

Make sure you set yourself up for a wonderful retirement, full of stress-free living, traveling, grandkids and hobbies!

CHAPTER 16
What's So Great About Roth IRAs?

With so many types of retirement accounts out there, what are the reasons people choose Roth IRAs if they qualify? And what does it mean to qualify for a Roth? Why do I think they're great? It's not like I can wear a Roth IRA to a cocktail party!

- First of all, let's go through some features of a Roth IRA:

- For 2021, you can contribute $6,000/year ($7,000 if age 50 or older)

- Contributions are made with after tax money. That means any money you put in a Roth has already had taxes taken out.

- Roth IRAs grow tax deferred which means you don't have to pay taxes on the growth every year. Also, the government doesn't make you take out a Minimum Required Distribution, starting when you're 72, like they do with all pre-taxed retirement accounts (401k, Traditional IRA, Rollover IRA).

- You can always take out your contributions penalty free, although it's best to let the money in the account until retirement; after all, that's why you're saving.

- If you wait until you're 59 ½ to take money out of your Roth IRA, you won't pay any taxes on the growth...ever.

- However, there are income restrictions, so not everyone can contribute to a Roth:

Filing Status	Modified adjusted gross income (MAGI)	Contribution Limit
Single individuals	< $125,000	$6,000
	≥ $125,000 but < $140,000	Partial contribution
	≥ $140,000	Not eligible
Married (filing joint returns)	< $198,000	$6,000
	≥ $198,000 but < $208,000	Partial contribution
	≥ $208,000	Not eligible

Married (filing separately)	Not eligible	$6,000
	< $10,000	Partial contribution
	≥ $10,000	Not eligible

What's so great about all this? Let's say you're in your twenties, just getting started and you're in the 15% tax bracket. Anything you're able to put into a Roth will be taxed at the lowest tax bracket—forever. Suppose you contribute $6,000 one year and leave it there for 35 years. At a 5% growth rate, you would end up with over $33,000. That means you would only pay 2.72% taxes on the entire amount: ($6,000 X 15% = $900) ($825/$30,000 = 2.72%).

If you were saving in a pre-taxed IRA, like a 401k, 403b, Traditional IRA or Rollover IRA, and had that same scenario as above. So now you're 60 years old and need to take out the $33,000 savings for living expenses. You're retired so you're probably also in the 15% tax bracket; however, you would now owe $4,950 for taxes ($33,000 X 15% = $4,950). See the difference?!

Moral of the story: people in low tax brackets benefit tremendously from long term growth in a Roth IRA.

Another big use for Roth IRAs comes when people retire. Since they don't usually have big incomes in retirement, they are in low tax brackets. That makes it easy to convert some of their pre-tax retirement accounts into a Roth IRA. This is called a Roth conversion. What some people try to do is convert just enough to stay in a low tax bracket so they're only paying a small percentage of taxes, then let it grow and use it as the last retirement assets since the government doesn't impose a

Minimum Required Distribution starting at 72. Keep in mind that they will pay taxes on the money they convert in the year they convert their assets.

Roth IRAs are also good for inheritance purposes since you're passing along assets that don't cause a huge tax burden. Many ways to use a Roth IRA, so if you qualify to contribute – do it!

CHAPTER 17
ŞAVING FOR ÇOLLEGE

I received a BS in Business Administration from Miami University in Oxford, Ohio. It's a great school and I had a fantastic experience; however, I would like to apologize to my Dad for some of the electives I took. My Dad was a single parent of four kids and yet I didn't have an ounce of college debt. We split the costs, so he paid for my tuition, room, and board. I paid for my books, entertainment, and travel costs. Obviously, he paid for the bulk of my education, so I feel bad when I reminisce about my karate, golf, ballroom dancing, and wine class for which he paid. Sorry.

College today is so ridiculously expensive. I'll never forget taking our son, Joseph, to Ohio State and listening to one of the administrators tell all the kids that it's okay to go into debt for your education. I wanted to throw a tomato at her. She should have said it's ideal to make it through school without any debt.

There are many aspects to this overpriced problem. Sometimes, the parents just want bragging rights about the school their child attends and don't pay attention to the cost. Sometimes, no one is talking to the student about the return on investment for the various majors. Spending $80,000 a year on a major associated with very limited job opportunities can suffocate your child with debt for so many years. Besides, why is it all right to loan an unemployed student tens of thousands of dollars? They certainly couldn't get a car or home loan on their own! Talk to them about the job prospects and typical income levels for their majors, as well as options on earning potential for majors that aren't connected with great earning potential. Then see if the price of their school is something that makes sense for that particular degree. Finally, since the government went into the college loan business, there's no reason for these schools to cut costs. The amount of college administrators making six and seven figure incomes has grown exponentially over the years. It's so disheartening that the colleges and universities aren't creative with cost cutting methods for your child to get their degree.

There are two types of accounts people use to help save for college. You don't need a specific type of account; however, they both have tax benefits which makes them appealing.

Custodial Account (UGMA/UTMA)

This is a uniform gift to minor account or uniform transfer to minors' account. This is basically a brokerage account in your child's and your name. It is funded with after tax money; however, any gains, dividends, etc. are taxed under the child's tax rate. Just like a general brokerage account, everything that happens in this account is taxed during that particular tax year.

Since the IRS allows this account to be taxed at the child's rate, they consider this money to be an irrevocable gift to the child. While the money in the account has to be used for the child's purpose, it does not have to be used specifically for college. It can be used for secondary schools as well.

You can choose any type of investment you'd like as you would in your general brokerage account. Just remember your goal and time frame. If college is only a couple years away, don't be super aggressive.

529 College Savings Account

These accounts are more restrictive but are wonderful tools for education savings. So-called 529 plans were previously only used for college education, but due to the 2017 Tax Cut and Jobs Act you can now use up to $10,000/year for K-12 private school expenses as well as $10,000 in student loan repayments. They are funded with after-tax money; however, any earnings in the account are tax deferred (you don't pay taxes on the gains every year) and if you use the money for education purposes, you never have to pay taxes on the earnings at all! They work very similarly to Roth IRA except they're for education and not retirement. Some states will even give you a state tax deduction. Plus, most of these 529 plans allow you to put a couple hundred thousand dollars in them.

The investments are also more restricted. Most 529 plans offer age-based portfolios which are self-adjusting portfolios. These portfolios are more aggressive the farther away your child is from college then they become more conservative the closer your child comes to going to college. They will also offer what they call "static portfolios." That just means the portfolios don't change on their own. If you chose an index portfolio, it will always be an index portfolio; it doesn't become more conservative on its own.

Let's say your child doesn't go to college and you've saved all this money. You can transfer the account into another child's (or relative's) name. They are transferable accounts. My husband and I have two children, but I only opened one account. Once my daughter finished college, I transferred the account into my son's name. If you don't have anyone else who can use the account and your child is definitely not going to college, you will have to pay taxes and a 10 percent penalty only on the earnings.

What if your child gets a scholarship? You are able to withdraw the amount of the scholarship without penalty, but you'll still have to pay taxes on the earnings.

Which Account is Best?

Some things to consider when you're deciding which account is best for your family. While custodial accounts are less restrictive, keep in mind that once your child becomes the "age of majority" according to your state (it's usually 18 years old), the account has to be put in their name and they can use the money any way they want! If they would rather buy a motorcycle, a leather jacket, and some spectacular riding boots instead of using the money for college, they can. Plus, even though you're paying taxes on the earnings at the child's rate, you're still paying taxes whereas a 529 is tax deferred and even tax free if you use it for education purposes.

529 plans are personally my favorite type of education savings, but since there are some restrictions, I certainly didn't put the maximum amount in the account. I basically used it to pay for tuition, room, and board but used my regular brokerage account savings for any other expenses like books and apartment rent once my kids were out of the dorms. Keep in mind that while college is certainly expensive, you were already paying for your child when they lived at home. They ate food, took showers, used electricity, and needed clothes so some of those costs are reduced at home and transferred to the college expenses.

However, my biggest piece of advice is to lower the cost of college as much as possible. One of my clients sent his son to the satellite branch of a major university and had him live at home for two years. His son had a job, worked and went to school. At the end of the two years, he transferred to the main campus. Their family certainly had enough money to send him to school for all four years. They wanted to give their son the money when he graduates to be able to get started in life with a car and savings for a home. It's not a bad idea. In my opinion, too much is made of "college life." Think of the electives I took!

CHAPTER 18
REDDIT WALLSTREETBETS AND BITCOIN

In the eighteenth century, women wore long sleeved wool gowns as bathing suits. Yes, wool bathing suits! Whose idea was this?! Can you imagine getting that wet and how hot you'd be lying out in the sun?! Over time and once spandex and nylon hit the market, wool bathing suits went by the wayside, thank goodness! So why would anyone invest in a wool bathing suit company knowing they would most likely go out of business? That's pretty much what's happening today with the Reddit WallStreetBets chat group that ran up the price of Gamestop, AMC, Nokia, and several other struggling companies. The pandemic, lockdowns, and changing shopping habits have hurt these brick-and-mortar stores, among others, so much that they're now some of the most "shorted" stocks on the market. So why would this Reddit WallStreetBets chat group be interested in investing in these companies?

Let's start out by explaining what it means to short a stock. Shorting a stock means you make your purchase backwards because you think the stock is going down. Short sellers like to profit from struggling businesses whose stock shares are falling. Some people find this practice to be unethical and unfair since the practice can really put downward pressure on a stock. Short sellers must initially borrow someone's share to sell. Then, when the stock drops, they buy the shares at the lower price. Instead of buying low then selling high like most people, short sellers sell high then buy low. As you can imagine, if you borrow shares to sell and the stock goes up instead of dropping, you could lose quite a bit of money. When this happens, these short sellers must "cover their short positions" by buying back in even though they have a loss. When there are so many short sellers covering their shorts, this can cause the stock to go up dramatically since there are many more purchases.

The Reddit WallStreetBets group of traders recently stuck it to the short sellers who are mainly from hedge funds and major investing firms. They started buying shares of companies such as Gamestop because these companies were heavily shorted. Once they started buying so many shares, the stock price climbed and then the short sellers had to cover their shorts. That caused shares of these stocks to skyrocket to amazing levels! Many of these short sellers ended up with huge losses because of this. Cheers to the little guy and they certainly are! They have a flippant attitude towards trading and many funny phrases like "sending it to the moon" complete with a rocket emoji. There are diamond hands and even ape emojis since apes are stronger together. They've actually managed to donate hundreds of thousands of dollars to save apes!

On one hand, kudos to this group for thinking of this strategy and sticking it to people who profit from others' misfortune. On the other hand, this is not fundamental trading and will not last. These companies are struggling to survive, many of them will go out of business. Typically, you buy into a company with strong growth prospects or one that pays a good dividend. While it's fun to watch, I would caution anyone looking to join in. Stick to the fundamentals and you'll be better off in the long run.

Bitcoin

There's a reason why I wanted to combine the Reddit WallStreetBets group and Bitcoin traders in one chapter. Neither one of them follows the fundamentals of investing and in both cases, the individual investor is the main player. Bitcoin is a cryptocurrency, not associated with any one country. There are other cryptocurrencies as well, it's just that Bitcoin is the most famous. They operate on what's called a secure, decentralized blockchain-based network. That's a complicated term that just means they don't trade through the stock exchange or even at a bank; they trade peer to peer. Basically, when you trade Bitcoin, you trade with another person or entity and you're the one responsible for your own currency. You are your own bank. You can trade this and others through apps such as Coinbase or now directly on PayPal.

Bitcoin is like anything that trades all day, it goes

up and down. The only problem is that it's very hard to predict what moves this currency. It's very risky because there aren't any indicators to study, just trading habits and price history. It's one of the least used, heavily traded currencies. People don't tend to buy goods and services with Bitcoin just yet, but they do trade it. That's not to say that it won't be used more in the future. It certainly bears watching. It's also been used in illegal activities, including thefts, so some safety nets would be a good idea. I'm not a fan of overregulating; however, some regulations do serve the purpose of protecting the consumer.

That said, there are people who have made money trading Bitcoin and swear by it. If you do decide to trade cryptocurrencies, make sure you know the risks and start out small. No need to put a huge chunk of money into something this volatile. Since there aren't many indicators, try to buy on a down day. Nothing goes up continuously and forever. For as many "take it to the moon" WallStreetBets and Bitcoin traders who have made money, there are by far more who have lost. Some have lost a significant amount of money. While I think it's a good idea to take calculated risk with moderate to long term money, these are very risky practices. Make sure you're using extra "play" money, just in case.

ABOUT THE AUTHOR

I was born in a small blue-collar town about an hour southeast of Cleveland, Warren Ohio. Not only was I the only girl out of four children, but my Mother passed away when I was 13 years old, so I was the only girl in my family, period. My Dad was left to raise the four of us alone. He came from a hardworking, family oriented, country loving, and of course, male dominated family.

There were five boys and one girl in my Dad's family and all the men were very successful businessmen. It was intimidating!

True to my family, I majored in business at Miami University. I married my husband, Bill, who was also a business major, and we had two children, Charlene (named after my Mom) and Joseph. After staying home with them when they were young, I decided to work part time as a trader on the phones for Fidelity Investments. I loved it! It was so energizing to work with clients and be a part of their financial decisions. When my children were older, I worked full time meeting clients face to face in the branch office. Naturally, I was one of the few women in the office. Here I was again surrounded by men!

During my thirteen years at Fidelity, I worked in a variety of roles, including trading (stocks, mutual funds, and options), stock plan services, new hire training, an Investment Representative, and an Account Executive, among others. This experience really helped me become well rounded and able to assist clients in various financial situations. I earned countless awards including Fidelity's highest award, President's Circle. It was a fantastic experience! However, the absence of women always bothered me. Most of the time if a woman came to a financial appointment, they were silent. They seemed intimidated and uninterested in something they will depend on their entire life! As a woman, I've had to fight for a voice among men in my family and career. I feel passionate about helping women find their financial confidence and voice.